Still Standing

by Elizabeth Stewart

© 2008 by Elizabeth Stewart. All rights reserved.

ISBN 978-0-6151-8769-3

Cover photo taken by author, © 2008

For Superman,

Who always dared me to live.

<3, WonderWoman

Consistency

I feel as if my words are constantly
banging with tiny fists
against the backs of my
eyelids, screaming,
begging to be let out.

Something is amiss, though
that I don't want to let them out.
I want to keep this secret, hold
it tight and hidden
and shout it out loud
at the same time.

I'm behind on everything except feeling.

Blindsided.

This is the feeling of the rug being jerked out from underneath you.

I have no feet.
I must,
I walked to work,
but I can't feel them,
can't feel anything
below the heart,
because if it's not there,
what use is anything else?

Just the buzzing in my brain
and the rattling of old forgotten thoughts.
Love and want are two different things.

Grind my teeth into dust
grip the handrail until
the bones in my hand crumble
let the saline behind my lids
dry out my eyes.

You can only get hurt if you let someone in.

Not true.
I get hurt all the time.
Toughen up, strange little girl.
You've got a long way to go.

Just remember: Love is a lie.

A day in the life of the Panic Disordered

Somewhere after Babcock
the train stopped short
for lack of room
and a handrail
within reach
I tumbled.

The Asian woman glared
the Jewish man muttered
the rest of the car stared
silently.

Behind my headphones
underneath an
unnecessary winter coat
my eyes glaze over
my skin flushed
furious embarrassed
defiantly terrified
red.

At Blandford, retreat.
Get off, skulk,
smoke at Kenmore
where my card can't
be read.
A few trains later
grab a seat.

Park Street
I put away my book -
Bukowski -
and I haven't
stopped sweating
yet.

The steps at
Government Center
and all the bricks
between the buildings
are rain-slicked wet
reflecting a perfectly clear

blue sky.

My credit card
refuses
to swipe at the 7-11
on State.

I whack my head
on the back wall of
the elevator.
Ten minutes late.

I've done a full day's work
before even getting here.

Not Knowing

I feel sick
panicked
crazed...

The irrational parts of me
are screaming,
laughing,
because to them,
I've fucked up, again...
And they just love to watch me fall...

Control is a funny thing
because I have
capacity for it
but not enough.

I miss him
and it hurts
like he ripped out my heart
and left a
gaping
bleeding
wheezing
hole.

My voice is shrill now
scrambling to make excuses
explanations
declarations

but The Others
are telling me
that that's what I get
for letting someone in
that's what I get
for trusting someone
that's what I get
that's what I deserve
"You are the mistake, here"
a sinister whisper
echoing in my empty head.

This is the inner dialogue
I never let anyone hear.

The not knowing...
that's what is worst.

NC-17

I'm broken and
damaged and
shattered and
bruised and above all
hurt.

Double standards are my way of life.

I want you
but I can have him
and him
and him, too.
Why not?

I don't value sex.
How can I?
How can anyone,
knowing how much it can hurt?

It's just screwing.
Just sleeping around.
Just fucking.
Just fucking
ridiculous.

From the first time.
I liked it, but
it scared me
because I knew it would
come back to
hurt
me.

And so it did.

And so I poison myself with it.
On my knees.
Tied to the bed.
Dressed up and
pushed up and
made up and
sexed up...

Slowly dying
trying to
be what they want
cause they'll
take it from me
anyway.

He did.

When will you?

Thought of the day

To the one who was too good to be true
(and was the one who got away):

I would be a whole lot easier to like - maybe even to love - if I weren't so
goddamned difficult.

All I can see are your pictures,
and you might as well
be a million miles away.

I'm not sure if it's everyone or
no one who feels this way,
but you are goddamned beautiful
and it makes my head spin.

Bruckner, 9th Symphony

I love you,
I whisper,
resting my head
on his shoulder,
leaning towards his neck,
between the third and fourth movements.

He rubs my back,
kisses my feverish forehead
before saying,
I love you, too.
He holds my hand
the whole time,
and wraps an arm around
my shoulder to guide me
down the marble stairs.

He's stoic.
So stoic in the face of the crowd.
I'm surprised at this,
but say nothing,
staring at his profile on the train.
This is it.
I'm pretty sure this is it.

Visit

I'm high on cold medicine,
curled up next to him, staring.
It's his hair, I think,
that's why I love him.
Flopped over to the side,
the serious look on his face while he writes,
the keyboard on my laptop
echoing too loudly in my sickly ears.
The big brown eyes framed
with long, long lashes,
the fingers to the lips while he thinks,
the furrowed brow.

I mutter and squirm as
I cough under my blankets.
He looks down at me,
eyes wide and concerned and rubs my cold arms.
I don't want to let him go.
I threaten to keep him
as I wrap my body around his.
But tomorrow he goes, just the same.
This works.
This feels right.
This is comfortable.
This is it.

We explored a bookstore tonight,
laughing over the psychology section,
how ridiculous all the self-help books seem
in the face of all our combined disorders.
Myspace for Dummies.
Idiot's Guide to Writing Erotic Romance.
Idiot's Guide to Social Anxiety.

I introduce him to Bukowski,
and smile as his eyes light up.
We share a few poems from
"What Matters Most is How You Walk Through the Fire" and he is
blown away.

We sniffle and cough together.
He reaches for my hands without prompting.

He knows when to touch me
and when to be careful with
wandering hands.
He nudges my shoulder for kisses.
My head fits just so on his shoulder.

He's skinny, but stable enough for me.

I can't help but think what happens next.

His smile is like being home.

Pachebel, Canon in D

I try not to cry
as I watch him walking away,
towards his train.
I fail.
Tears escape despite my efforts
I walk backwards for a bit,
trying to decide whether to
watch or to just leave.
I decide to just leave.

Get out as soon as I can,
so I don't collapse in
this puddle in shivering,
feverish hysterics.

I push through a crowded South Station,
go out the doors on the other side,
my hands shaking as I pull a cigarette from my purse.

He'll be back, I try to calm myself.
He says he loves you.
And has given you no reason to doubt.
I can barely taste the cigarette for all the mucus.
I'm not crying. I rarely cry.
I'm out of tears. But I'm so sad.

His eyes. I think I will miss his eyes the most.
The way they looked at me
 like I was something
precious and valuable.
Worthy, I think.
Like he would treat me as a treasure.
Like he would take care of me.
This is how I should have been looked at all along.
This is how I should have always been treated.

I collapse on a bench in the T station.
A street musician is playing classical guitar.
My hands feel so lost without his to hold.
I don't know what to do with them.
I sniffle, wipe my nose, steel my face against the crowd.
He'll be back, I remind myself. I hope he'll be back.

I'm not ok in this body.

I think if I keep saying that,
maybe the higher-ups
might hear me
and issue another.

But I'm not ok
And I won't feel guilty
for trying to escape.

And a great escape it will be.

Pull the fire from my eyes
and the spirit from these cold numb lips
Take the tendons from my knees
to see how far I bend
Rip my heart out of my chest
because we know it still beats

however lopsided.

My biceps scream in pain
from the outside
while I lay prone
and try to not roll on them
and shiver
in pain and chilled.

The kitten keeps
a watchful eye
from his
protective post
atop my legs.

Streetlight, Street bright

I live on a street with a broken glass front door.
Lonely cars preaching bumper sticker doctrine.
A broken bicycle wrapped around a bent street sign.
Stained sidewalks from overextended partiers.
Garbage spilling off the curb and into the gutter.

It's ugly here.

But its home.

What would yours read?

Do you ever wonder about that one person?
Not the
"one that got away".
Everyone has one of those.
Some of us are one of those.
No,
I mean the
"too good to be true"
person. Of either gender.

I'm having a hard time
delineating between
"best friend,"
"confidant," and
"unrequited crush".
I was supposed to give up that last one a long time ago.
Is it terrible of me to be head over heels and still have this flicker in the background?
I'm sorry.
He doesn't always get it.
Or maybe he does, all too well.
Few people illicit tears in the same way.
I have the feeling that
if everyone in the world
would have a sign, mine would read,
"Help."
and his would read
"Ask me."
Or maybe,
"Let me."

What would yours read?

Changing gears

I love you like an old country song.

With cowboy hats and long
stretches of empty highway
on a lonely moonlit night
in a rumbling pickup truck

Running through the fields
and into the woods
chasing butterflies and
dandelion fluff
all smiles and laughter

Something pure and real
true to both our broken hearts
healing as the soft summer rain
sweetening the smell of fresh cut hay

And slow dancing to the
steel guitars

It feels like home with you.

Interview

My hands smell like
copy paper and cigarettes with
bitten-short nails and
kitten-play scratches.

They're shaking.

Misplaced notes and
misplaced routes

On the train to
nowhere
no doubt.

Five stops.

Here we go.

Autumn Falls

The trees are still green
But the sky is dark white
Overcast with clouds
While Black-Eyed Susans lay
Down to the wind

Things are changing
No one takes the time to notice

When is it my turn to change?

Can't get out of bed today

Lay perfectly still
If you don't move
you won't explode
and the world won't end
And maybe you won't cry.

Pulse
pulse pulse
Nothing to do but
Listen to thickened blood
Pounding through her veins
And thumping in her ears
Pushing pain around
A body that doesn't
Deserve it

And every beat
Gets us closer to death

Alumni

September hit, and there's a noted change in tone.
The students are back, and I'm farther and farther away from that life.
The air is colder, my mind is gone.
But it's nice to reminisce.

Maybe this is happiness:
Wearing a heavy cable sweater and
drinking french vanilla coffee with
hot cocoa mixed in and
staring up out of the skylight at
the beautiful crisp blue New England sky and
wondering what that boy is doing or
wishing he was here but
loving him no matter what.

Love a rainy night

It's raining in the street, but not on the sidewalk, it seems,
Save that for those with headlights and wiper blades.
The sidewalk is safe
Hunched girl, rounded, hiding, watching, with a cigarette and flitting eyes everywhere...
They don't see her
They never do

Good figure in the shadows
Round bottom
Sturdy, strong top

Of the world
And crumbling fast
Collecting cigarette cartons and broken hearts
In her tiny cluttered basement ivory tower

Everything is wrong
Mixed up, crazy
For no reason

She slips behind the shadows
The doomed world
Keeps losing her
Grip

Except that one thing
That makes her darkened heart smile

To Superman, II:

Crazy is coming back.
I'm obsessed with it.
This black, blank feeling, comes from nowhere
What self-indulgent crass girl am I to say this?
And I'm off again
Reading, scrambling for books that tell me why I am the way I am, with characters that are crazy like me, novels and nonfiction and first person accounts...
Watching movies and pointing out scenes, I understand that, that's how I am, that's what I want to do...

(I'm glad I'm a chicken
Or my arms would be ribbons)

But it's never quite the same, is it?
My crazy is not like yours
The way we sit up all night, writing away, but saying nothing.
And sleeping around and not feeling anything.
Having everyone fall for you without reciprocation
Without any reason
Without any logic
Isn't all it's cracked up to be...
When you're crazy.

Why?
That is the everlasting question.
And it will never get answered.
No matter what, no matter how many of us die on its account...
No matter how many of us are dead inside.
Why?
Help.

Streetrat

She sees them.
Walking down the street.
It makes her nervous.
Men, boys, with their leering,
lecherous eyes and dismissive glances.
Long for attention.
Hate it just the same.

What would they say, do?
What would she do?
If she could stay still.

Lonely.
Not the desperate, clinging, passing lonely.
The deep-seated, awful, heart-wrenching feeling of being alone.
If anything happens... what do I do?
Am I enough?

I'm lonely.
And I like it.

Like those scabs I can't stop picking at, the scars I retrace.

I feel the life draining out of me.
I was not meant to live this long.
I am living on borrowed time, and so every misstep and every mistake is closer to my own demise.

Laid the blade flat on my face tonight.

And then what do I do?
I don't know.

Melancholy.

That's the only way to describe this.

Waiting for inspiration...
or the other shoe to fall?
I'm not sure.

I cannot get my inner judge to stop.

Of course, I have not yet identified it,
so I will need to do so as soon as possible,
 in order to quell it's progress.

Give it a name,
a face,
embody it,
anthropomorphize it,
whatever.
Because then it exists,
and then,
that much easier to destroy.
It is not just delineating
right from wrong.
Our conscience does that much.
The internal judge,
like the courtroom judge,
interprets that which the
conscience decides is law.
It is that part of us that
filters,
stops,
pauses,
hesitates,
waits.
It is the bits that
confuse us to the point
of needing to say
"I don't know,"
the thing that blocks that knowledge,
wisdom,
enlightenment
from truly being made known to us.
Every moment has one,

and most moments move past
the judges without a second glance.
But I have let mine get out of control.

It is not that no one else is good enough for me.
I am not good enough for myself.

"Are you sure you're not Buddhist?" she asks.
Philosophically only.
And even then,
mostly only regarding the escape
from this plane of reality into
Nirvana,
enlightenment,
understanding,
peace.

I believe that the philosophy of religion
is more important than the ritual.
Because we can only have ritual
through philosophy,
put into practice.
Although, if I really were Buddhist,
there would not be a
"self" for which I
"should" be good enough.
New works

I am hungry for new writing.
It is like being hungry, with all manner of food surrounding, and not know what your body or mind is craving.
Something to spark my own.
Something that invokes feeling.
All my favorites, from various places, are fading away, and thus, I fade with them.
Have I changed enough to be this woman?
Have I moved on from those romanticized days?
How do I remove the roadblocks set up by my judges?

I need it to be autumn soon.
Something about the way the light slants and shines cool and calm keeps my soul at bay.

Grey areas

"The beautiful thing
about standing in the grey area, love,
is that I see both black and white."

It's one of those days.

Where I'm gloriously sane and
lucid, and
all those things I've
written about before.

But I see the other side.

For no other reason
than
I've been there myself.

Is it wrong that
I kind of want to go back?

A week's worth

Dancing with cigarettes outside the bar.
He does smoke like an old man:
fingers straight,
face elongated.

"Relax that hand," I want to say

"You're not as crazy as you make yourself out to be, you know," he says.

Smile.
"Caught me on a good day,"
out of the corner of the mouth,
with a sly look sideways.

"You're not that bad either.
You're not that big of a freak.
You're actually kind of cute.
Be proud of who you see in the mirror."

Sincerity?
Perhaps.
Not "that" crazy?
Sure.

Holding back the tears before speaking.
Bite the lip.
"It's not like they didn't say that."
"Oh."

Swing, up,
down,
brain twirling and
disconnected.

The bottles sit in the backpack,
untouched, for how many days?
Counting, thinking, being sure.
Words won't come out.
Haven't for days.
Is that worrisome, to sit
at this keyboard and
stare at a blank screen

for hours?

Nodding into the phone,
forgetting they can't hear that way.

Staring at the phone,
wishing he would call,
knowing that he won't.

Free agent,
being pushed off on everyone else.

This week. Sure thing. Doubtful.

Dye the hair, fit back together.
Make it real.
Not that crazy.
Sitting nearly fully clothed
in the shower while blue water
drips down around
a bowed head.

Just turn up the music.

am I talking?

i'm holding my tongue
because you're holding my heart
and i fear that if i am a disappointment
with one swift move
you crush what keeps me alive

i know you're not like them
i know this time is different
but i have heard that line before
and i'm sorry i'm being so careful
i know i don't disappoint
(you, at least
only myself)

i shut down the other night.
silence, confusion, the works.
it's like i'm testing him,
making sure he's in this for the long haul.
fishing for compliments because i know he'll hand them out like candy...

i want to give my best to you
but i realize that i don't have a best
i've given it away
and others have taken
what didn't belong to them

but you didn't fall in love
with the smiling put-together girl
from a long time ago.
you fell for me when i was
broken but healing

i still need concrete answers
when, where, how long?
forgive my childish ways.
what does forever mean?

is that my heart flying
at the words you say
or panic rising in my throat

because no matter what i tell you
i still doubt?

Ok today

i've opened this window
three times today
just to shout
to my world
about
how much i love you

up and down
in and out of
love
is a fleeting thing

and more often
than not
i lose it
without knowing how

today
however
i revel in the
thought of
my name
on your lips
pressed to my ear

like someone
patient
sweet and dear
could fix
my brokenness

Yeah, ain't that a kick in the teeth...

This is different.
Any other time, any other person,
I would just walk away.
I've done it.
I watched myself do it.
Can't walk away from this.
So I stand here,
holding the bag
that is now holding
the remains of my heart and
soul and
other assorted innards,
wondering what the hell happened.

My lack of faith in myself
will always be the problem.

Pro Life?

It's different when it happens to you.

Reading testimony from a person -
a product of rape.

"Counseling and therapy can help heal,"
she writes.

[And I can tell she's female
from the emotion in her words.
"Emotion won't win over fact."
That's what they keep telling me.
So why not here?]

Not if one can't access it.

And single motherhood?
Poverty?
Lack of healthcare?
Lack of options?
Unstable environments?
Resentment?
Isn't that a shame, too?
Set me up to fail, why don't you.

I didn't choose to live.
To be born.
To have this name
this face, these hands
these eyes,
this mind.
Someone else chose
all this
for me.
So now I'm doomed to this
miserable life.
Where everyone else
is allowed to
is expected to
make my choices for me.

It's different when it happens to you.

More Panic

something is squeezing me,
wrapping around me,
nothing's around,
but it's getting
tighter
and
tighter.

not in a good way,
not a comforting way.

i think its panic.

i'd panic if it was anything else.

is death coming so soon?

Cursed.

I want more pain.
Yes,
I want more pain.
I wake up to it,
the craving,
the carving.

It's never enough.

I've dreamt about
sex
this night
and last,
about being -
well
you know -

because it isn't enough
that it happened just once
no
I have to relive it
every time the lights
go off
every time the clothes
come off
every time that I
get off

because I'm never sure what
they want
from me
let alone if
I should like it.

FUCK you
for
FUCKING
me
over
for the rest
of my pathetic
life.

There's a special place in
Hell
for people like you.

So I want more pain.
I want more Hell
I want more of it now...

so that when you die...

(and God, I wish
I could be there
to
see
your
last
miserable
breath)

you get
all this
for eternity.

Bones

His bones stick out so sharply
from his hips
his knees
his elbows

I'll break him.
And his hair is longer than mine

But his hands are gentle
and his kisses are perfect
and I could be safe in his eyes
forever.

Expectation

it's work.
the panic is back.
it was quiet when he was here,
quiet when he left,
quiet on the weekends
and the holidays and the
times that i go home.
it's work.
but i'm afraid it's any work.
not just this.
not just this office.
i've never been able to see past the next five minutes.
because that's all we have.
and no one is willing to see that.
i have no future.
because it's right here
being crushed under expectation.

one of my lovers
has cystic fibrosis.
he's 24.
his life is more than half over
and he's got interesting
brave theories
of living with an inherited
genetic
terminal
illness.
the way he lives
says it all.

I hate what this
has done to me
but I cannot
separate it
from myself
because it is me.
cf is not his fault.
but nor is depression
mine.
just something
we die

with
and live
for.

i'm being crushed
by
expectation.
the idealism -
that tomorrow
will be a better
day.

but i'm not sure
i'll live
through
this
one.

Beautiful boy

three nights
i've slept in
my dirty sheets
our dirty sheets
that smell like
you like
me
like us
our sweat stained
sex stained
bad-chinese-food stained
muted red
sheets
with pillowcases
full
of tears
and
the thought of
being curled up
on my side
with your hand
on my back
while you,
beautiful
boy,
with shining
sincere
dark eyes
whispered secrets
no one told me before
and while we
giggled under the blankets
at the timing of that
bad commercial
that still couldn't ruin
the mood
nor would a
leaping
playing
bouncing
chaperoning
kitten

i think it's ok
that you haven't learned
about that spot on my neck
or the one on
the inside
of my hip
because you have a
head start
on permission to touch
my ears
and a lifetime to learn the rest.

What I am made for:

poetry words sentences
stories memories kisses
snuggles sleeping
kittens music
listening playing
walks in the rain
sleeping in hallways
sitting in strange cubbyholes
standing on the bridge
long hot baths sheets out of the dryer
sweatshirts jeans sneakers
cigarettes and soda
books poems [of others]
poetry [my own]
being on my knees
being good with my mouth
being good with other certain anatomy
smiles photos [that i'm not in]
photos [that i take]
grammar debate intellectualism
immaturity beauty truth
love
leather satin cotton fleece
reading candles
quiet company
silence
solitude
hugs

What I am paid for:

none of the above.

Declaration:

Dreams don't
come with commitments.

But
"I love yous" –
they do.

Scene I – Things I wish I could say

"Dammit- I wish I could believe you.
I really do.
You have no idea.
I don't know if anything you've ever
said to me has been the truth.
Just stop lying to me.
I'm tired of it.
But look at me...
look at me now.
I look better,
I sound better,
I feel better than
I have any time since knowing you.
I finally know I'm gonna be ok.
And I'm sorry.
I can't let you back in.
You had your chance –
and you messed up.
And I've forgiven you.
But I'm not God.
I'm only a human.
I cannot forget.
I'm sorry.
I have to be strong for me.
We always try to go back to the old.
Newness scares us.
We go back to the hurt,
to the pain,
to the things that we know
aren't right...
simply because we know them.
But that doesn't make it right.
And this isn't easy.
You've cut yourself out of
the picture.
How am I supposed to glue it back in?
Why is that my responsibility?

You know- if you had asked me to... I would have spent forever with you.

Scene II – Things I should say

You don't have to
be afraid for me
anymore.

I'm really gonna be ok.

I see that look you give me
every time that song
comes on the radio.

It was true a long time ago.
Heck, it may be true now.
But not in the same desperate,
pleading way.

I've figured a lot of things out.

A lot of things are right now.

Trouble was,
they had to be wrong first.
And I don't like being wrong.
It scares me.

I'm sorry I dumped on you so much.
It seems somewhat silly now,
but I had this weird,
hero-worship crush on you.
You were always
listening to me whine and
telling me that things were ok.
I clung to that like it was my
last breath.

You cared.
It didn't feel like I got a lot of that before you,
even though
now I know I did.
Thanks.

The edge

I have been to the edge.
I have been to hell and made it back.
I have seen the darkness.
I have been in the darkness.
And I hated it all.
All the while getting there, I could not feel the slide. But suddenly, the only place I could look was up. At where I had been.
I was too far gone to reach for help. No one noticed I was missing anyway.
Suddenly, a voice.
"My child."

I cowered in fear. I knew who it was. I knew what the voice could do.
I waited for it to say more.
Suddenly, I felt lighter. I saw light. Felt warmth. How...?
Blinking my eyes in the brightness, I squinted upward, then looked quickly down. I cannot live in this place.
"Yes. You can."

My feet were placed firmly on the ground, a safer distance from the edge and the sloping hole.
It took awhile...
But soon, I was dancing wildly... overjoyed to be returned to where I belonged.

Tidbit:

sometimes,
i wonder
what the purpose
in being
a beautiful soul
is
when it's
obvious
that people
don't
care.

Mistress

Music is my mistress...

Oh, God, she's a bitch...
But I am a whore for her graces...
Her beauty.
Her passion.
Her life.

I want so desperately to please her, to make her mine completely.
Sometimes, she loves me.
Sometimes, she is cold and distant, and I almost forget about her.
Sometimes she flees.
But she always comes back.

Always.

There are days when I hate her.
When I wish she would just go away.
When I wish we had never been acquainted.

But somehow she makes me forget that pain.

And like old lovers, there are no lines, no boundaries.
We just are.

Together.

She gave me her life.
I am forever indebted.
I play servant to her every whim.

She is overbearing
cruel
manipulative
aggressive

addictive

But I love her

Words

Oh, God, how I wish I had the gift of words.
Not words to tell you what my day was like.
Not words to express the petty feelings each day brings.

Words to make you go, "oh..."
and wonder about life.
I wonder about it myself sometimes...
The ones that reflect beauty.
I know there is beauty in the world.
Let me share it with you...
The kind I love to read myself.
If only I had the time.
If only I had the talent.

But I sit here at this keyboard for hours on hours.
I can barely make my
exhausted hands,
arms,
body.
punch out the words
I need for classes.
My weary eyes barely stay open,
ideas flying past them in my head.

Oh, they're in there.
I have the will
I have the way
But finding the two together on any given day?
good luck...

See what this has done to me?

How easy it is to be emotionless so suddenly!

Losing Touch

Is this what it's like to drift apart?

Where is this going, anyway?
Anywhere we want it to, love.

Forward would have been nice...
I hope I still have that chance.

Do we?

Fuzzy

the blank page is daunting
daring me to spit out the words
and stop them from bumbling about in my brain

we went out for coffee last night-- matt and i
they celebrate six months together this weekend
we get our caffeine fix and browse barnes and noble
chatting briefly about this book and that cd and those dvds
then to eat n park
talk of issues
home
news
but expertly maneuver around the ones that fill the room
the pink elephants
see how they dance!

"i'm old enough to know what love is.
this is it.
i'm in it."

on the way home-
"i tried so hard for so long to not be gay"
i say nothing
then "mark's a good kid"
"yes- he's wonderful"
i hide my jealousy behind the happiness that he's found his other
his muse

is it crazy that i can't read and comprehend anymore?
i sat outside for a smoke and played with the ashes
wondering if it would still hurt if i just dug the orange butt into my wrist
like i'm superhuman or something
like it wouldn't hurt
i think id be surprised when it did

if i don't feel something soon, i might lose it
the numbness is nice
but only for awhile
id like to have something to feel again
the bell jar has started its descent

i don't want to feel like i was before this

soon ill be stuck behind a wall of glass
only an observer
silent again
to those outside
how can i observe from inside?

i know my silence drives others mad
blame chris for this one
i got so good at sitting and staring
taking what he dished out
or ignoring him but not really
wanting to cry every time he
put me down
called me stupid
just because i believed

all i want to do is run away and write and write and write

will i always be afraid of the words?

Fun new facts:

so what you're basically saying is...
eating disorders are ok,
as long as they're
high browed
high priced
and have a specific name
with 'diet' attached to the end of it

great.

i prefer the old fashioned method of hating myself.

much more effective.

i hate you
because you don't have a mind for words
and you don't realize
or even think that
proportioned can mean balanced
and balanced does not necessarily mean
equal all around

i hate you
because your politics
reduce and twist
my words to mutated theory
so there is nothing beautiful about them
(or me
but didn't we know that already?)

study the language you live in
for the love of god
and maybe you'll understand it someday
and respect it

I'll send you a dictionary
along with my regards

go to hell you ignorant bastard.

or maybe just

fuck off

would be a better epitaph

Philosophy

i don't feel so trapped today

i should sit on the end
then i could write and it would look like i was taking notes

my [hand]writing was a lot better in christology

she wants to make us better 'writers'

NO

i don't want her messing with my creative mind

i AM a good writer

i don't want to become faceless and lose myself in
the technical and research writing

i want my own ideas

no quotes
no books
just let me tell my story

or someone else's....
(he doesn't exist- you know that, right?)

You give me fever

things i wish could say were real

my head rests on his chest
i love to breathe him in
and listen to his heartbeat
lull me to sleep

my body curls next to his
warm and comfortable
arms around me
one hand in my hair
the other on my back

beautiful
so he says
i duck my head
i still don't believe it

i move, just a bit,
and wake myself

it was just a dream.

I woke up

sat straight up in my bed
thought i slept through the day
but i beat my alarm

then i remembered

i stumbled to the computer
looking for your words
hoping it was true
for once a dream
was real

aren't i the fool to think it might be?

to think you changed
to think you can trust
to think...
at all...

i can't change anything
even though i want to
i thought...
it was different...
no.

i have to start the day
knowing
my dreams about you may never come true...

Think myself to sleep in poetry

I'm laying on the edge of the bed
My stomach hurts
from the abuse it's taken lately
or from nerves because
you're right behind me?

Your hand knows just where to go
and rests perfectly at my hip
I relax

Sleep

Later

Entwined in your body
Safe and warm
You reach for my hand
and our fingers entangle themselves

you may have created a monster
and now you have to keep her satisfied

Smile in the dark

Sleep

If I were invisible:

if i don't move
they wont see me
and what a fake i am
and how much like them
i really am

re-entry is hard
and i forgot about that
i'm used to young and fast and
trying too hard
i forget that some don't try

why can't i just shrink
away to nothing
be invisible
just a spirit
wandering
loving

because that's what
i'm supposed to do
and i can't
not like this
not in this shell

i'm smaller than my body gives me credit for

first, love yourself...

god, i'm trying

I think the house is blowing away

i can't stop watching him.

"yeah. i do what i want."

i bet you do.

his skin tastes so good.
his five o'clock shadow is rough under my tongue.

i miss his lips on mine.

maybe someday.

maybe someday, i'll start saying what i want.
maybe someday, he'll stop teasing.
maybe someday, it could work.

maybe someday, i'll wake up.

"you always remember your first kiss," they say.

especially when he stares you
in the face
day
after day
after day.

i wonder what goes on behind those wide eyes. what do you think when you stare at me?

Pieces of you

that night
those days
double camp chairs
trigger happy tv
rice stuff
scrambled egg
that stain
the night
your bed
your couch
my apartment
those glasses
that pleather jacket
the adidas cologne
that suit
your green eyes
big nose
blonde hair
trench coat
forerunner
lakeside house
big dog
my friends
your job
in english
i don't understand polish
not the way you want to be
drifting
falling
love
hate
love
hate
hit
hurt
fight
friends
her
that time
those girls
the diner
long drives

garbage bags
dripping snow
romeo
juliet
out the window
cold
worried
scared
scarred
don't leave
go away
where are we going
your shaking hands
bite your lip
drumsticks
practice rooms
stop watching
don't listen
leave me
love me
don't
green pants
red shoes
deep voice
white teeth
devils smile
emo
bubonic plague
have to write
away message
letter
don't read
please understand
dirty room
dirty dishes
keep me busy
keep me here
not like that
phone calls
late nights
long days
hard lives
i can't
you can

run away
alone
lies
hurt
anger
grow up
grow up
no regrets
keep going
far away
stay
stay there...

sweep them all up, throw them away.

Exhausted, but write it anyway:

and so my heart ends up
in your hands
and i am trusting you
with its every beat
my most precious part
now belongs to only you

please be gentle
as you always are
but hold it firm
and do not let me slip away

for you have given me
your heart just the same
and if i run
i take
this piece of
you with me
because this is meant to be
whenever
where ever
however
it will be perfect

hold my heart and
hold my hand
and come with me
and i with you
and listen to the hearts beat

Cranial leakage

my heart hurts.

i get this warm and safe feeling
when i talk to you
but you're far away
and i am here
and the feeling disappears
when you do
and there's nothing we can do
about it

but would you really feel this way
if you were here
if you knew me
the real life me

i'm nothing special
you know that, right
i'm messed up
but don't let on

self medication
either hurts or helps
anesthetize my self
(i forget there is no self)
or amplify the pain
of which there is much

you want to save me
rescue me from myself
and just hold me tight
i know

i didn't care about him
and knew it
and stopped the proceedings
before they went too far
because all i wanted was you
and i didn't know how
to get to you

and what about her

do you still love her
am i a distraction
is this real
more real than that
or am i just new and different
and exciting because of it

you don't love me
or are too shy to say the words
and even then
what does it do
how do you know
how do i know
and what do we do about it

It's not you.

tie me down and tell me i'll be ok.

its not you that i'm afraid of.
i scare the hell out of myself.
doing my inner monologue of constant worry.
just shut up.
let me be.

its not you its me.
i'm putting the running shoes back on.
tie the laces together
so i fall into your arms
and don't get anywhere.

what if
no longer exists.
i banish it from my vocabulary.

no regrets.

just go with it.

Mechanic

So often,
I feel like I am the
mechanic for change.
That I am merely
setting things into motion –
especially for other people,
the ones that need it most.

That my purpose lies in being
a catalyst for upheaval.
To be for others the one
who causes and/or witnesses
that "moment of clarity"
where lives change and things
happen and realizations are made.
Do I dare bring freedom, thought, difference?

Perhaps this is why I do not "fit" anywhere.
Make waves,
then get pushed away by them
before I see the final outcome.
Other's success comes at a price.

(And I can't help but think,
"Have I really made a difference?
Do they know?
Who will set the wheel in motion for me?
Who will make me realize?
Who will change the course of my life?
Who will make a wave for me?")

This is the role I have defined for myself.

Run away with my heart

Did you mean it last night when you said I was beautiful?
Did you mean it when you said you'd considered us?

I hear it in your voice...

When you said softly "you know we wouldn't work," it sounded more like you were trying to convince yourself more so than me.
But then you say you want me, too, and why does that confuse me?
Because I'm not supposed to want you back.

Why am I the one you call-- even for the little things?
Why am I worth it?
Or am I really worth it?
Is this because I might be gone?
Is it because someone else might have me?
It is, isn't it?

You haven't lost me. I'm still right here. But he's here, too, in my heart.
Both of you have special places there.
But now what?
I'm afraid to make any move, because I could lose you both.

Our song:

[Did you know that was the day I fell in love with that group (again)?]
Driving around in your car, speeding down the highway.
Not wanting to question where your heart really was, and believing it
could, eventually, just maybe, be with me.

And when I lost it, you looked at me, every time it played,
because you knew when I sang along, under my breath,
I meant it, I was trying to tell everyone what was wrong and
how to fix it.
You listened, but never tried to fix it.
Others mattered, not me.

[And everywhere I turned for weeks after, there was that song.] Nerves
and smiles, and wondering "what the hell am i doing?"
Amidst this chord, those rhythms, that feeling that I get when I listen to
them. Making up the harmonies as I whispered along, not wanting to
reveal that I actually can sing.

It's cheesy, I know, but I actually believe(d) in that song. And I know
that's how you felt, too. Like you yourself wrote it, just for me.

All of these, and only one remains...
I never wanted any but this.
This is right, this is true.

Limits

I am fascinated by language and its limitations.
Certain aspects of life just can not be explained in the patterns of speech
and writing.
"Things got really bad..."
"It's too hard..."
"There's nothing there..."
The inconsistency of language astounds me,
how there's no REAL way to say:
I care
This is special
I am hurt
I don't understand
I love you

[new thought, same day, same class:]
Why do I feel like I know everything already?
I know what is good
What is right
What, if anything, is true
There are sparks of good in all
There are flashes of evil in every moment

There just is.

Into Ploughshares

How do we end a war these days?
Why have we stared something
we cannot finish and
that only hurts us?
Do we just walk away?
Pretend nothing happened?
Do we stay to clean up the mess we've made?
Why can we spend billions a day on
devices that only destroy,
maim and injure and kill –
and cut programs to aid the poor in our own country?
And what of education?
Can we not spend our money on
teaching children peace?
What about faith?
Or love?

Never underestimate the power of habit.
Social systems and structures
are flawed from the very beginning.
Like any educational tactic,
we must unlearn what we
know
and program a
new response.

But are we even aware of what we do?

Who will wake us up?

Doubting Elizabeth

what if i hurt you?
what if i run away?
why am i scared of being stuck?

why do i still feel your arms around me?

what do we know about life?
what will we do with ourselves?
why do i cry now?

why am i a jerk?

is it really your arms i feel or the chains of being tied down?
can i really wait for you?

In the eye

i can't look him in the eye cause
i know why i'm here
and part of me just again got shy
but the other part wonders
when did i get like this
still another part wants to cheer me on

i can't look him in the eye cause he knows it all already
and if he doesn't he'll figure it out because this is what he does
but i'm on high alert all day afraid to move afraid to look afraid to breathe
wrong or someone might know
know what
i wasn't ok when you asked me
i was trying not to run away
i was trying to slow everything down
and make my head stop rushing and not thinking
i'm never ok
but sometimes things slow down and can be enjoyed
or if you distract me with a wall of jazz music
while i stare at it and
wish i could be one of them behind the glass case
and i'm trying to avoid my own eyes
they're the only thing i like but i can't look at even them today

but its hard to do that when you look at me like that
i can't look you in the eye when i say i know because i'm not sure i do or
trust it its hard to know when you feel like this about yourself did you
hear the tears behind my voice until you made me laugh
but i know you mean it

Loud and clearly

playing my guitar
a song comes on
that i don't know
i pause and listen
then sing along

words don't matter
i'll sing nonsense
but the melody from my lips
resonates the body
and the guitar
the strings move one by one
as i lilt on those notes

recognize a group
by the themes repeated
might be a music major
if
you can't listen to music
the same way everyone
else does

you hear things
and know things
and want things
that no one knows about

and understand more
than what the song
means to most
because you live it
and breathe it
and become the song

but no one's supposed to know...

next song comes on
and i pick along
and sing
the room rings
everything the song begs

Maintained

i'm not high maintenance
in the regard
that i need tons of time to get ready.
or that i need a million beauty products
to slather on before i go out.
or that i'm a picky eater
(as long as it's not red meat or seafood or mushrooms and
as long as you don't watch me pick at my plate).
or that i'm picky about what we do and where we go...

i'm high maintenance insomuch that...
don't ask me that question yet; i'm obviously not that girl
don't look at me that way, it makes me nervous
don't touch me there.
or there.
or there.
OR there.
better yet, don't touch me at all.
don't laugh like that
don't act like that
don't.
just don't.

Quick before work that no one will read

its out there
if you want it
take it and run
i've already given it to you

but i don't think you want it

who would
its been beaten around so much
its not much to have

i should stop hanging so much hope on you
because i'm pretty sure you don't want me
so i'm not allowed to want you like that

and if we name it
would i run away again?

but if you were me

in this situation

with me being you

what would you be thinking?

Hold

he's holding a place i'd rather him not.
rather than saying,
hey don't touch me there,
i don't like that,
i am wiggling, twisting away from his grasp.

he is trying to catch my eye and
i am trying to avoid his.
he loosens, but doesn't let go.

so calmly he says,
i guess then that this is a part of your body you don't like so much?
i whimper a negative tone and wriggle some more
and he stage whispers
i don't mind.
but my mind screams
please no no nonono i want to be perfect and
you're finding out i'm not
i want to be a tiny tiny little package for you
instead of everything hanging out and jiggling and nono...stop...
he must hear the catch in my breath and lets go and smoothes his hands
over my back in a hug while i cling to him.

you don't talk much. i want to know all that is inside your head.

but i don't even want to know all that is inside my head.

Untitled night

my shampoo
his cologne
a camel turkish silver

his arms around me
lips to mine

and the wine

I like

when i
drive home in
the morning and
i can still smell you and
your cologne on me
everywhere and
it stays on my clothes all day.

i also like tequila

even if it gives me hangovers that wake you up.

Life moves quickly

forget the fairy tale stuff
this is hell or high water
and damn
the tide comes in fast

Empty

I know.

Rage.

I've done it before.

I've needed it like that.

I raged against the world
inside and out
echoed howled protests against
the winds

of change.

But there comes a point
when rage
doesn't do it anymore.

Anger only multiplies
and hatred divides.

Someday, the rage is gone.

The past is the past.

Maybe it hurts.

But there is nothing left
for you
because you emptied yourself

wasting

music
on deaf ears
and beautiful art
on blind eyes

The forest fire consumes and destroys
frightening and powerful

but also brings life
through charred remains
and nourished soil.

Wall

I can only get so far.
And then I hit a wall.

It's always there.
I don't know if it will ever go away.

But I keep pushing on it.
Maybe it will fall over.

Maybe this is a good thing

she lights up
only for
admiring the
grace of her hands

its been awhile
since they've felt
graceful

but she can't bring
herself
to poison
herself
anymore

her hands will
have to be
graceful
with only
the rings

maybe the right spark
is back
in the smoke
for the music calls
her

Thursday

The philosophy draws me in

but I can't write it down

and so it is lost

I want to play
I always want to play
but the daggers in
my wrists
say otherwise

I miss that feeling
that feeling of being a part
of something so imperative
to love
to creation
to expression
to life
to everything

This is all I have to be
dramatic about
not a dream deferred
a dream disgruntled
and disenheartened
disenchanted

And I wonder if I can
even still
through the pain
and memories
does my body remember
how
and
why
it was pushed so hard
far
and held so high
can my hands still hold it

do my muscles remember

my heart does.

It's spring.

It fires through my hibernating body,
and burbles up to lighten tired eyes.
Spring is easy to love,
Easy to be in love
I'm lucky I am
I am alive
The wind is still cool,
but the sun...
The sun!
My winter-chapped hands reach for it.
And for you.

Take the A train

Jazz can only be understood
through my tilted head.
Straight up is just sound.
Watching intently hands
and faces for the
expression so familiar-
And yet, so far away
Do I dare make my way back again?

And when I leave you
sliding out of the bed
(I can't help but wonder
why
this, us, me.)
in early morning or
late afternoon
I take the train
away from you.
Straight up its just
a hand to hold
a body to hug
an ear to whisper into

So I tilt my head.

Playtime

Come and play in my bed

Crawl into my arms
(into my heart)

Move just that way
Make yourself comfortable
I surprise myself by
being comfortable

Breathe into my ear
let me hold onto your arm

(I) Play with your chain
while you play with my hair

You wanted to come,
I note, to myself

Wondering where the next step
Next play date
Next L(...)

This is just fun...

Naps

Confused.
This is for you...
I do this for you...
You're here for me?

Sighs, moans, screams
I love your hands.

I can't sleep still next to you
Reveling in safety
Don't want a moment to slip by
Unnoticed

Kiss my hair
and hug me tight
Are you sure this is alright?

You're so tired
Dark circles
Don't work so hard, Superman

Sleepy smudged eyes
and sleep-ruffled hair
I still turn you turn me on

Cocooned

Sunday has always been
the most hopeless of days.

I burrow under the covers
in sweatshirt and pjs,
piling more and more on top,
feeling their weight comparative
to the weight on my mind.

Living alone is hell,
in the summation of Don Miller.

I'm beginning to believe it.

In autumn, even the wind can feel still as death.

After

The towers have nothing
on the fall my heart takes
when you say
"I'm not sure when"
or
"maybe"
makes my chest
collapse on itself

I like you too much
that, I know
But even friends make time for each other.
Even if they're
not in limbo.

So what would you have me do?

It's easy

it's the kisses
down the chest

it's the hand
behind my neck

it's kneeling to the side
hands brush my hair aside

where did you learn that?
how, if...?
before i can think...
there it is...

it's always the same...
the process,
my name...

the empty feeling
after
and being held in, no,
for
a fleeting moment
new, old, first, last, many, few...

we're all easy.

Write it.

have you ever felt
that if you don't
write
or draw
or paint
or take photos
or create
something
that you would explode,
that you would physically die?

because i do.

Bad dream

he's back
and i can't say no

i want to fight him
beat him
hurt him
more than he hurt me

but instead
nod, smile
let him touch me

now every time i close my eyes, he's all i see.
and i want to die
rip out my eyes
throw up
cry

cold...

so cold...

never thought my bed wouldn't be my safe place

Quiet

men are always so shocked...
so surprised...
so appalled
when i tell them what has happened to me...

but men
(just like that)
have done this to me...

Remember

i remember when it was good.
when it felt right.
when it didn't hurt.
(so many things in my life fit this description)

i'm not used to actively cutting things or people out of my life.
i'm better at burning bridges without realizing they're on fire.
but you had to go.
you were bringing me down.
or was it a setup?
just to watch me fail.

he hurt me.
he HURT me.
god fucking dammit, HE HURT ME.
and i can't tell anyone.
what image am i really protecting, no-- hiding, here?

Blank.

Why can't I write?
Have I run out of things to say?
Surely not.

Liz.
Libby.
What is my name?

None of them look right.
None of them sound right.
None of them feel right.

Elizabeth.
Liz.
Libby.

I am someone different for
Everyone I meet
How interesting, the dynamic
nature of human
being
always moving always
changing
names homes goals lives...

Nomad

Tempered

Mother Earth
Is teasing us,
with sunlight
and warm breezes

Reminding me
There's hope
In January.

the beauty, but mostly the mess

Seeing my body
for what it really is
Hurts.
Even the good parts.

How I'd love
to go back
to Victorian times
Where ladies wore armor
of whale-bone and crinoline

And all men were proper
and innuendos were sweet
and revealing more than
a wrist
or an ankle
was shocking.

Ensconced in petticoats
I could hide
[from]
myself.

Will I always be this way?

Damaged goods.

Two steps forward,
three steps back.

Empowerment
never meant
to be so weak.

"I'm not right
I'm not fine

Flash:
He shouldn't
But..
I...
No
This isn't right...
Why can't I stop?
Why won't he stop?
Why can't I stop myself?
Guilty
I'm guilty too
NO
Why am I crying?
What do I do?
/Flash

"Out, out, damned spot!"
Dirty. Disgusting. Flawed.
Damaged goods. Explosive. Flammable.
And cracked.

Tuesday

The second hands on your clocks don't match.
The two face off,
one that I can see,
and the other hidden
somewhere to my left
that only you can see.
My foot twitches to the galloping rhythm.
I sit in silence for fifteen minutes,
twisting the cord of my iPod into every knot I can think of.
Occasionally, I glance up over the edge of my glasses. Purposely, so your
face is a blur.
I wonder where that viney plant came from,
on your filling cabinet.
It's been there for a couple weeks now.
Maybe a month.
I've lost track of time.
You try to probe, gently, like you do.
Closed ended questions aren't going to work, here.
"Is there..." I shrug.
I don't want to talk about it.
I know you're probably right.
My knee hurts where
I've crossed my legs.
My foot twitches.
I stare at the drawstring ties
on the bottom cuff of my pants.
I hate them.
On the way here,
I dragged them through puddles
and across the mud.
I sit in silence for
the last five minutes.
By the time I start the walk home,
I realize the tightness
in my shoulders,
the tension
across my back.

I've been sucking in, not holding back.

No, Not Kansas

Coughing so hard, I can barely stand up,
I wish I didn't have to hold the railing on the train.
Looking at tired eyes through
my sad ones,
what do these people do?
Think of?

Dorothy smokes a cigarette
outside the 7-11,
in Ruby Slippers
and fake fur.
We're not in Kansas anymore, Toto...
Toto is missing.
Maybe why she smokes.
The wind whips up State Street,
right off the harbor,
biting into feverish cheeks.
Close the eyes against the feeling,
see his eyes,
rip them open again.

Another day, another few dollars.

April is cold and grey.
Tearing up at work at least daily.
When does the unbreakable break?
Where is the line,
when does the splinter infect itself?

Taking up space.

Silently.

Last

Watching others,
my size or more,
avoiding their eyes.

Bellies out,
proudly(?)
displaying that which
they cannot hide.

Last acceptable prejudice.

Can't hide it.
Others can hide fatal flaws.

But me, my shoulders curl forward
and up.
Hips roll back.
Tummy sucked in,
booty tucked under.
Torso collapsing on itself.
Disappear, big little girl.
Makeup smears
as I wipe dry my eyes.
Purple eyeliner bruises.

Hear it from you

My heart hurts.

Do I still have one?

I give it away too often.

Playing with fire. Bound to get burned.

Fast. Too fast. Stop. No, don't. Good. Just like that.

Laying in the bathtub
 is the best place for thinking.
Fully dressed in the
cold empty tub.
Arms crossed across the chest.

The tub is narrow.
I am wide.
Enclosed, encased.
Almost a comfort.
Lean against cheap porcelain.
Body cools quick, shivers.
Funeral.
Casket.
Note:
No pillow. Double chin.
Wait.
Organ donation. Cremation.

Stare down the cat.

Does it hurt? Does it always hurt?
Will I always be waiting for it to hurt?
People hurt each other. All the time.
God, don't let me be one of them...

Don't flinch.
Don't pull back.
Pull down the walls, let someone in.

How do I explain this one?

Nor'easter

Black polish,
purple eyeliner,
black shadow crayoned on.
Black sweater.
Cigarette.
Outside matches in.

Breaking all the rules.
Who made them up, anyway?
Time to make my own.
Explore new things, people.

On the edge of a breakthrough.
Not getting better.
Just getting me.

Cold front off the ocean
(why can't I be on the other one now?).
Rain, grey, drip.
Wind whips through that tree I like,
kitty-corner my block.
That one that's been so broken.
Evening light glows behind its branches.

Competitive drive

Keeps me alive...
[one more day, I dare you...]

and kills me...
[I bet you can't...you aren't... you won't...be worth it...]

Feel very small today.
Not sure how that happens,
because I know I am not.
Small on the inside.
Another day of silence.
I wonder what the count is.

Let down your hair

Everything is touching me, digging in, too hard.
I hate it. I want it to go away.
But I do not want to be naked, exposed.
I went out today. Aunt dragged me to an event.
People hugged me.
Took pictures, hope they came out, shook and could not focus eyes.
I am slanty, twitching, ready to fall off the edge of the earth.
I cannot feel my feet on the ground
Ready to fly away
I want to give up.
Rest. I need rest.
I need it all to stop.
Cold hot zap zap
Cannot give up
Not yet

Born into the wrong time period
Parks in the city just aren't the same thing
Run wild in the fields
On the back of a strong horse
Lords and ladies and codes, not standards, of living

Live in a turret
and let down my hair
for Prince Charming
or Mr. Right.

would you risk the thorns in your eyes just to save me?

Scream

How
many
times
must I
scream,
"I love you,"
before I realize
it falls
on
deaf
ears?

B-line Hines to Harvard Ave.

You were the
most
adorable girl
I have seen in a long time.
Those eyes!
White dress,
black vest,
and this amber spider brooch
or pin
or button
or something,
but with your friends,
a guy and a girl.

I loved the Brat Pack
bow in your hair.

I wished I wasn't
so new at this going after
girls thing,
cause I was trying not
to stare and failing miserably.

You're absolutely beautiful, and I hope you know that.

-The blonde girl in the bright green PA shirt.

Stand Up.

I know it's hard for people
to wrap their brains around
what happened.
But I still don't understand it.
Knowing and understanding are separate.

It happened.
It sucked.
It still sucks.
But I'm still standing.

www.ingramcontent.com/pod-product-compliance
Lightning Source LLC
Chambersburg PA
CBHW032005080426
42735CB00007B/511